THE MENENDEZ BROTHERS

in a
nutshell

*A Quick and Concise Overview of the
Shocking Crime That Captivated America*

Felix Grayson

MINDSPARK
PUBLISHING

For the seekers of simplicity, the curious minds who crave the essentials without the fluff—this one's for you. Here's the story, in a nutshell.

"Brevity is the soul of wit."

— William Shakespeare

"Simplicity is the ultimate sophistication."

— Leonardo da Vinci

"Any fool can make something complicated. It takes a genius to make it simple."

— Woody Guthrie

IN A NUTSHELL'S PURPOSE

To provide quick, engaging overviews of pop culture, history, and trending topics, making it easy for readers to get the gist of any story.

IN A NUTSHELL'S MISSION

To deliver concise, entertaining content that educates and satisfies the curiosity of our readers and listeners in an ever-changing world of popular culture.

IN A NUTSHELL'S VISION

To be the go-to source for quick, digestible insights on the people, events, and trends shaping our world.

IN A NUTSHELL'S CORE VALUES

Simplicity: Making information clear, concise, and accessible.

Curiosity: Encouraging exploration and learning about diverse topics.

Entertainment: Providing facts in a fun and engaging way.

Timeliness: Keeping up with current events and trends.

CONTENTS

CHAPTER 1: THE MENENDEZ FAMILY – BEHIND CLOSED DOORS **15**

The Early Lives of Lyle and Erik 16

The Menendez Family's Wealth and Status 18

Family Dynamics – Parental Influence and Allegations of Abuse 20

CHAPTER 2: THE CRIME THAT SHOOK BEVERLY HILLS **23**

The Night of the Murders – A Detailed Account 24

The Police Investigation – Initial Theories and Suspicions 26

The Aftermath – The Brothers' Behavior and Public Perception 28

CHAPTER 3: WEALTH, PRIVILEGE, AND SUSPICION **32**

Lyle and Erik's Lavish Spending Spree 33

Public and Media Reactions – How Wealth Shaped Perceptions 35

The Turning Point – Why the Police Turned Their Focus to the Brothers 38

CHAPTER 4: CONFESSION, ARREST, AND THE LEGAL BATTLE 41

The Confession – Dr. Jerome Oziel's Role 42

The Arrest – How the Brothers Were Finally Taken In 44

Preparing for Trial – The High-Stakes Legal Strategies 46

CHAPTER 5: THE FIRST TRIAL – JUSTICE OR MEDIA CIRCUS? 50

Trial Proceedings – Prosecution vs. Defense Arguments 51

Media Coverage – Turning a Trial into Entertainment 53

The Hung Jury – Why the First Trial Ended in Mistrial 56

CHAPTER 6: THE RETRIAL – A DIFFERENT OUTCOME 59

Changes in the Retrial – What Was Different This Time? 60

The Conviction – Life Without Parole 62

Public and Legal Reactions to the Verdict 64

CHAPTER 7: LIFE BEHIND BARS – THE MENENDEZ BROTHERS TODAY 67

Adjusting to Prison Life – From Wealth to
Incarceration 68

Marriages and Relationships Behind Bars 70

Appeals and Ongoing Legal Efforts 72

**CHAPTER 8: THE LEGACY OF THE MENENDEZ
CASE** **76**

The Case's Impact on Discussions of Abuse and
Justice 77

Media and Pop Culture – How the Case Continues to
Fascinate 79

Changing Perceptions – Modern Re-evaluation of the
Brothers' Actions 81

CONCLUSION **85**

INTRODUCTION

In the summer of 1989, the quiet streets of Beverly Hills were shattered by a crime that would forever change the lives of those involved and captivate the nation for decades. The brutal murders of José and Kitty Menendez in their lavish mansion sent shockwaves through the community, not only because of the crime's sheer violence but also because of the identities of the perpetrators: their own sons, Lyle and Erik Menendez.

What followed was a saga that unfolded in the public eye, turning the Menendez brothers into household names and igniting a media frenzy. From the opulence of their upbringing to the chilling details of their parents' deaths, the story had all the elements of a gripping drama. Yet, it was far more than just another high-profile murder case. It was a story about family, power, wealth, and the dark secrets that can lurk behind closed doors.

The Menendez case raised questions that resonated far beyond the courtroom. Were Lyle and Erik victims of an abusive household, pushed to commit an unthinkable act in a desperate bid for survival? Or were they ruthless killers, driven by greed and a desire for control over their parents' fortune? Over the years, the case has been dissected and debated, evolving into a complex narrative that continues to provoke discussion and intrigue.

This book aims to explore the many facets of the Menendez brothers' story, from their privileged childhood to the trials that would come to define them in the public consciousness. We will delve into the crime itself, the psychological and familial dynamics at play, the media's role in shaping perceptions, and the legacy that endures to this day. Through this journey, we will uncover how this case forced society to confront its views on abuse, justice, and the human psyche.

As you turn these pages, you will find a story that is as much about the American legal system and media culture as it is about the Menendez brothers themselves. It is a story filled with complexities, moral dilemmas, and enduring questions—one that, despite the passage of time, continues to fascinate and challenge our understanding of crime and punishment.

CHAPTER 1: THE MENENDEZ FAMILY – BEHIND CLOSED DOORS

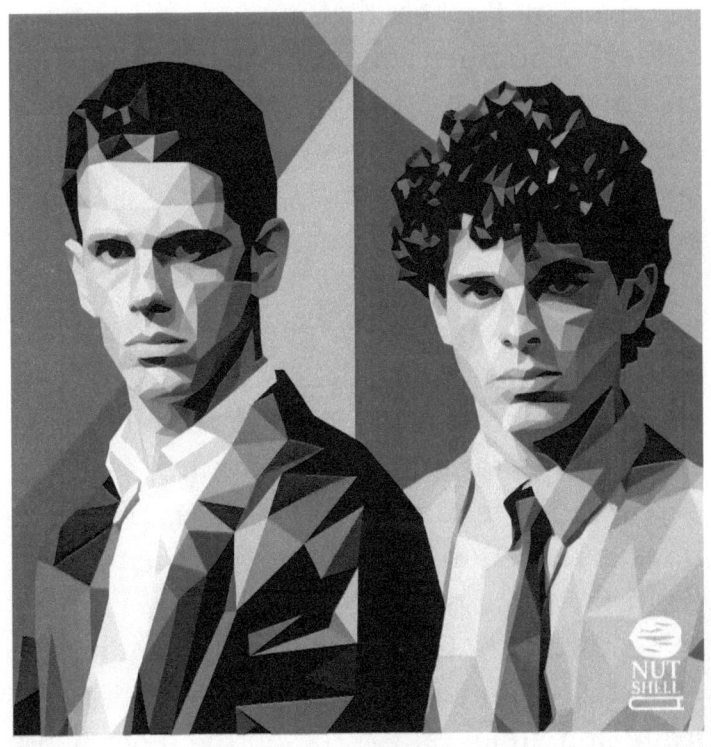

The Early Lives of Lyle and Erik

Lyle and Erik Menendez were born into a life of privilege and opportunity. The older brother, Lyle, was born on January 10, 1968, followed by Erik on November 27, 1970. Raised in the affluent neighborhoods of New Jersey and later Beverly Hills, the brothers' early lives were characterized by the best that money could offer — private schooling, summer camps, and elite sports programs. Their father, José Menendez, was a successful businessman with a drive for success, while their mother, Kitty, was a former beauty queen turned homemaker.

From a young age, the brothers were groomed for success. José Menendez, an immigrant from Cuba, had worked his way up through hard work and determination, becoming a highly successful entertainment executive. His ambitions extended to his sons, and he instilled in them the same desire for excellence. Lyle, as the eldest, bore the brunt of his father's high expectations, often pressured to excel academically and athletically. Erik, on the other hand, was more sensitive and artistic, with a natural talent for tennis that was fiercely encouraged by his father.

Despite their outwardly privileged upbringing, cracks began to appear in the seemingly perfect façade of their lives. Lyle was known as the more assertive of the two, often embodying his father's drive for dominance. Erik, in contrast, was quieter and more reserved, struggling under the weight of the expectations placed upon him. Their childhood was marked by relentless pressure to succeed, often leaving them in the shadow of their father's ambitions. The brothers' different personalities and their struggles to meet their parents' standards would later become a focal point in understanding their actions.

The brothers' early lives laid the groundwork for what would become a tumultuous family dynamic. Beneath the surface of wealth and opportunity, they were exposed to the darker aspects of their upbringing. As they moved into adolescence, the tension within the Menendez household began to mount, setting the stage for the tragedy that would unfold years later.

The Menendez Family's Wealth and Status

The Menendez family's wealth played a significant role in shaping their lives and the events that would later capture the nation's attention. José Menendez was a self-made man who had achieved the American dream. His career began in the hospitality industry, and through sheer determination and a sharp business acumen, he climbed the corporate ladder to become an influential executive in the entertainment industry. By the late 1980s, he was the president of Live Entertainment, a prestigious video distribution company. This position not only provided the family with a lavish lifestyle but also placed them in the heart of Beverly Hills society.

The Menendez home was a 9,000-square-foot mansion in one of the most exclusive neighborhoods in Beverly Hills. With its grandiose architecture, tennis courts, swimming pool, and luxury furnishings, the residence was a symbol of the family's success and status. Lyle and Erik were accustomed to this world of opulence, where they attended the best schools, wore designer clothes, and drove expensive cars. Their father spared no expense in ensuring that they had every advantage in life.

However, with this wealth came a certain level of scrutiny and expectations. Lyle and Erik were not just children; they were, in many ways, extensions of their father's image. Their successes were seen as reflections of José's achievements, while their failures were viewed as personal affronts to the family name. This dynamic created an environment where appearances were paramount. The family's social circle consisted of other wealthy and influential individuals, adding pressure on the brothers to conform to a standard of perfection that was both publicly and privately demanding.

Kitty Menendez, a product of the same upper-class world, struggled with her own issues amid the family's lifestyle. Despite the outward appearance of the perfect homemaker, Kitty grappled with depression and insecurity, exacerbated by the pressures of maintaining the family's status. Her emotional turmoil added another layer of complexity to the family dynamic, creating an environment that was, at times, volatile and fraught with tension.

As the family climbed the social ladder, they became increasingly isolated within their wealth. While to outsiders, they seemed to embody the pinnacle of success, inside the walls of their Beverly Hills mansion, the pursuit of status came with a cost. The lavish lifestyle masked deeper issues that would soon surface, casting a shadow over the Menendez family's fortune.

Family Dynamics – Parental Influence and Allegations of Abuse

While the Menendez family's wealth afforded them a life of privilege, it also hid the troubling dynamics at play within the household. At the center of these dynamics was José Menendez, a man whose relentless ambition and authoritarian parenting style left a lasting imprint on his sons. His desire to mold Lyle and Erik into his vision of success often translated into intense pressure, control, and a lack of emotional warmth. José's parenting was marked by strict discipline, high expectations, and an insistence on perfection, creating an environment where the brothers were expected to excel without question.

This section of their upbringing would later become the crux of the defense in their trial: the brothers alleged that they had endured years of psychological, physical, and sexual abuse at the hands of their father. According to their accounts, José's need for control extended beyond their public personas, seeping into the most private aspects of their lives. The abuse, they claimed, was a well-kept secret, perpetuated by an atmosphere of fear and silence within the family.

Kitty Menendez's role in the family dynamic was complex. As a mother, she was seen as both a caretaker and an enabler. Her struggles with mental health issues and dependency on alcohol reportedly made her a passive participant in the family's dysfunction. Lyle and Erik described her as emotionally distant and often complicit in their father's actions, creating a sense of betrayal that compounded their sense of isolation. They felt trapped in a world where appearances had to be maintained at all costs, even if it meant enduring unimaginable suffering behind closed doors.

The allegations of abuse would become a pivotal point in the Menendez brothers' trial, serving as both an explanation and a justification for the horrific actions they took on that fateful night in 1989. Whether these claims were entirely true, exaggerated, or strategically constructed by the defense remains a topic of debate. However, what is clear is that the Menendez family was far from the picture-perfect image they presented to the world.

The combination of José's domineering nature, Kitty's emotional struggles, and the allegations of abuse created an environment that was toxic and volatile. For Lyle and Erik, their home was not a sanctuary but a battleground—a place where wealth could not shield them from the darkness within. This section of their story provides crucial insight into the motivations behind their actions, illustrating how deeply family dynamics can shape one's psyche, for better or worse.

CHAPTER 2: THE CRIME THAT SHOOK BEVERLY HILLS

The Night of the Murders – A Detailed Account

August 20, 1989, was a quiet Sunday evening in the affluent neighborhood of Beverly Hills. Inside the grandiose Menendez mansion on Elm Drive, however, a scene of unimaginable horror was about to unfold. The night began like any other; José and Kitty Menendez were relaxing in their family room, unwinding in front of the television after dinner. Lyle and Erik, who had spent the day together, entered the home just after 10 p.m., armed and ready to carry out an act that would soon stun the nation.

What transpired in those few minutes remains one of the most shocking crimes in American history. Lyle and Erik approached their parents with shotguns they had purchased days earlier. Without warning, they opened fire, starting with their father. Lyle fired the first shot at close range, striking José in the back of the head. As the elder Menendez collapsed onto the couch, the brothers continued to fire, ensuring that their father was dead. Kitty, who had been asleep on the couch, was jolted awake by the noise. In a frantic attempt to escape, she tried to flee but was mercilessly shot in the leg, causing her to fall to the floor.

The brothers did not stop there. In a terrifying display of brutality, they continued to fire at their mother, shooting her multiple times in the arms, chest, and face. The carnage lasted only a few minutes, but the scene left behind was one of unspeakable horror. The room was drenched in blood, the furniture splintered from shotgun blasts, and the bodies of José and Kitty lay motionless amidst the wreckage. When the gunfire finally ceased, Lyle and Erik stood over their parents' bodies, their lives forever changed.

What happened next was a calculated attempt to cover their tracks. In an effort to make the murders appear as if they were part of a botched mob hit, the brothers removed evidence and left the scene. They drove to a local movie theater, purchased tickets, and attempted to create an alibi. Afterward, they returned home and made a frantic call to 911. The voice on the other end was filled with hysteria as Lyle screamed, "Someone killed my parents!" The call marked the beginning of a case that would grip the nation.

The Police Investigation – Initial Theories and Suspicions

When the police arrived at the Menendez mansion, they were greeted with a gruesome scene. The sheer violence of the crime initially led investigators to believe they were dealing with a professional execution, possibly linked to organized crime. José Menendez, with his high-profile career in the entertainment industry, had made powerful connections and a few enemies over the years. This line of inquiry seemed plausible, and the police began their investigation with this theory in mind.

However, as the investigation progressed, certain details failed to align with the notion of a mob hit. The brutality of the murders, particularly the excessive number of gunshots, seemed excessive even by organized crime standards. Additionally, there was no sign of forced entry, and nothing appeared to have been stolen from the home. These inconsistencies raised questions about the true motive behind the killings.

During the initial investigation, the police interviewed the brothers, who seemed grief-stricken and traumatized by the loss of their parents. Lyle and Erik recounted how they had discovered the scene upon returning home from the movies. Their performance of shock and despair convinced the police, at least temporarily, that they were devastated victims of a horrific crime. In the months following the murders, the case remained unsolved, with investigators struggling to find solid leads.

As time passed, however, suspicion began to shift toward Lyle and Erik. A breakthrough came when friends and acquaintances of the brothers noticed their seemingly unusual behavior in the wake of the tragedy. Within weeks of their parents' deaths, Lyle and Erik had started spending lavishly, buying expensive cars, jewelry, and clothing, and even planning elaborate trips. Their spending spree raised red flags, particularly given the context of their parents' violent deaths. The brothers' sudden access to their parents' fortune and their extravagant lifestyle began to paint a different picture, leading the police to reconsider their initial theories.

Adding to the suspicions were rumors of a troubled family dynamic. As investigators dug deeper, they uncovered accounts of tension and strife within the Menendez household. Though these revelations did not directly point to the brothers as the murderers, they provided a potential motive that contradicted the mob-hit theory. Despite the growing doubts surrounding the brothers, the police still lacked concrete evidence to link them to the crime. The case, therefore, remained shrouded in mystery, awaiting the crucial piece of information that would crack it wide open.

The Aftermath – The Brothers' Behavior and Public Perception

In the months following the murders, Lyle and Erik's behavior raised eyebrows not only among those who knew them personally but also in the public eye. The men's sudden change in lifestyle seemed to clash starkly with the image of grieving sons. Lyle, in particular, embraced his newfound wealth with enthusiasm. He purchased a Porsche, invested in a restaurant, and even moved into a luxury condominium in Marina del Rey. Erik, while somewhat more subdued, joined his brother in extravagant shopping sprees, buying Rolex watches and designer clothes.

To outsiders, their behavior appeared bizarre and callous. How could two young men, who had just lost their parents in such a violent manner, immerse themselves in such conspicuous consumption? Some speculated that the brothers were merely coping with their grief in an unusual way, using money as a means of distraction. However, as time went on, more people began to view their actions as suspicious. The stark contrast between their public demeanor and the brutal crime raised questions about their involvement.

Despite the brothers' efforts to appear as victims, cracks began to show in their story. Lyle's emotional breakdowns seemed exaggerated, often occurring at opportune moments when he was in the public eye. Erik, on the other hand, appeared more withdrawn, struggling to maintain the facade of a devastated son. Friends and family members who were close to the brothers noticed subtle changes in their personalities. Lyle became more aggressive and controlling, while Erik showed signs of increasing anxiety and guilt.

The media quickly picked up on the story, transforming the case into a national spectacle. Television programs, newspapers, and magazines featured extensive coverage of the "Beverly Hills Murders," focusing not only on the grisly details of the crime but also on the lives of the two brothers. As public interest grew, so did the scrutiny of Lyle and Erik's actions. They became figures of fascination—young, wealthy, and now at the center of a high-profile murder investigation.

Public perception began to shift. The brothers, once seen as tragic victims, were now viewed with a mixture of suspicion and intrigue. Was their behavior simply a reflection of privileged young men acting out in the face of grief? Or was it the manifestation of deeper, darker motives? The case quickly evolved from a horrific crime into a psychological drama that captivated the nation. As investigators closed in, it became increasingly clear that the brothers' story was not as straightforward as it initially appeared.

The turning point came when the police received a tip from a surprising source: Dr. Jerome Oziel, the brothers' therapist. What he revealed would send shockwaves through the investigation and set the stage for one of the most sensational trials in American history. But before the world would hear their confessions, Lyle and Erik would continue to live their double lives, haunted by the secrets they struggled to keep buried.

CHAPTER 3: WEALTH, PRIVILEGE, AND SUSPICION

Lyle and Erik's Lavish Spending Spree

In the months following the brutal murders of their parents, Lyle and Erik Menendez began to engage in what could only be described as a spending spree of unprecedented extravagance. To onlookers, it appeared as though the brothers had suddenly been released from a financial restraint, eagerly indulging in luxuries that went far beyond the grieving process. Within weeks of their parents' deaths, they spent an estimated $700,000, signaling a radical shift from mourning sons to two young men basking in wealth.

Lyle, the older of the two, seemed to dive headfirst into this new lifestyle. One of his first major purchases was a sleek black Porsche Carrera, a status symbol that was quickly followed by even more lavish expenditures. Lyle moved into a luxury condominium in Marina del Rey, decorating it with high-end furniture and technology. He also took a keen interest in the restaurant business, investing in a trendy new establishment called Chuck's Spring Street Café. The restaurant became a symbol of Lyle's transformation, from a college student to a businessman seemingly overnight.

Erik, while initially more reserved, soon followed suit. He invested in tennis lessons and entered professional tournaments, living out a dream that had been overshadowed by the demands of his parents. Together, the brothers bought Rolex watches, expensive clothes, jewelry, and even sports equipment. They traveled, staying in the most luxurious hotels and dining at upscale restaurants. The money they were spending was part of their parents' substantial fortune, which they had inherited after the murders.

Their sudden and conspicuous spending was alarming, especially given the recent violent deaths of their parents. While some might argue that Lyle and Erik were simply acting out of emotional distress, using money as a coping mechanism, others saw their actions as deeply troubling. The extravagance suggested a kind of freedom, a release from the control their father had exerted over them in life. However, as the spending continued, it became increasingly difficult for observers to reconcile their behavior with that of two sons supposedly devastated by their loss.

The brothers' spending habits would later play a critical role in the case against them. Not only did it suggest a potential motive – the immediate access to their parents' wealth – but it also provided the police with a trail to follow. Their luxurious purchases, along with their increasingly public displays of wealth, began to attract the attention of investigators who were already starting to question the circumstances surrounding the murders.

Public and Media Reactions – How Wealth Shaped Perceptions

The Menendez brothers' spending spree did not go unnoticed. News of their lavish lifestyle quickly made its way into the media, transforming the public's perception of them. In the immediate aftermath of the murders, Lyle and Erik had been seen as tragic victims, two young men who had lost their parents in a brutal act of violence. However, as their spending habits became more widely known, the narrative began to shift. To the public, they no longer appeared as grieving sons but as privileged heirs squandering their parents' wealth.

The media played a significant role in shaping this perception. Sensationalist headlines splashed across newspapers and TV screens, painting Lyle and Erik as the poster boys of greed and excess. Stories of their extravagant purchases – the luxury cars, high-end condos, and designer wardrobes – became fodder for public discussion. The contrast between their newfound lifestyle and the brutal crime that had unfolded just months earlier fueled suspicions about their true involvement in their parents' deaths.

The case quickly evolved into a debate about wealth, privilege, and justice. To many, the Menendez brothers epitomized the excesses of the ultra-rich, individuals who, despite their wealth, had become ensnared in a scandal that highlighted the darker aspects of privilege. The public's fascination with the case was not just about the murders themselves, but also about the brothers' behavior afterward. It became a story about how money could potentially corrupt morality and cloud the pursuit of justice.

As media outlets covered the brothers' every move, a narrative began to emerge. Lyle and Erik were portrayed as two young men who had lived under the thumb of a domineering father, only to erupt in a fury of violence once they gained their freedom. This image was complicated by the brothers' sudden access to their parents' fortune. For many, the idea that they could be both victims and perpetrators was difficult to grasp. Public opinion became polarized: some believed they were entitled brats who had committed the ultimate betrayal for financial gain, while others saw them as troubled individuals driven to an unimaginable act by years of familial strife.

This public scrutiny intensified the police's interest in Lyle and Erik. The more the media covered their lavish lifestyle, the more suspicious they appeared. The police began to question why the brothers would behave in such a manner if they were genuinely mourning their parents. This growing suspicion would soon lead to a deeper investigation, turning the focus squarely onto the Menendez brothers.

The Turning Point – Why the Police Turned Their Focus to the Brothers

The Menendez brothers' spending habits and the public's reaction to their newfound wealth were pivotal in shifting the focus of the police investigation. Initially, detectives had considered various theories, including the possibility of a mob hit or a burglary gone wrong. However, as they observed Lyle and Erik's behavior, a different scenario began to emerge—one that involved the brothers themselves.

The turning point in the investigation came with the brothers' extravagant expenditures. Detectives began to piece together a timeline of their activities following the murders. They noted how, within days of their parents' deaths, Lyle and Erik had started spending large sums of money. While it wasn't illegal for them to access their parents' estate, the timing and extent of their spending raised suspicions. The investigators began to view the brothers' actions as indicative of a deeper motive: the immediate financial freedom they gained after their parents' demise.

Adding to the suspicions were the interviews conducted with friends, acquaintances, and family members. Many of those close to the brothers reported that Lyle and Erik seemed unusually calm and composed in the weeks following the murders. Some friends recounted conversations in which the brothers appeared more interested in their newfound wealth than in finding the perpetrators of their parents' deaths. Their apparent lack of fear or concern for their own safety — despite the violent nature of the crime — struck investigators as particularly odd.

As the police dug deeper, they uncovered further inconsistencies. The story that the brothers had provided about their activities on the night of the murders began to unravel. Forensic evidence from the crime scene, combined with witness statements and the brothers' own behaviors, gradually pointed to them as prime suspects. Yet, the police still lacked concrete evidence directly tying Lyle and Erik to the murders.

The breakthrough finally came when the police

learned of the brothers' sessions with Dr. Jerome Oziel, a therapist whom they had confided in following the murders. What they revealed during those sessions would become the cornerstone of the prosecution's case against them. But before the full story would come to light, the brothers continued to live their double lives, spending freely and seemingly unburdened by the gravity of their actions.

This shift in the investigation marked the beginning of the end for Lyle and Erik's facade. As the police zeroed in on them, the public watched in anticipation, eager to see if the suspicions swirling around the Menendez brothers would ultimately lead to their downfall. The stage was set for a legal battle that would capture the nation's attention and challenge perceptions of wealth, privilege, and justice.

CHAPTER 4: CONFESSION, ARREST, AND THE LEGAL BATTLE

The Confession – Dr. Jerome Oziel's Role

The unraveling of the Menendez brothers' facade came through an unexpected source: their therapist, Dr. Jerome Oziel. Following the murders, Lyle and Erik Menendez sought counseling, ostensibly to cope with the trauma of losing their parents. However, their sessions with Dr. Oziel would soon take a shocking turn, revealing the dark truth behind the brutal crime.

The brothers' decision to confide in Dr. Oziel marked a critical point in the case. Initially, they appeared to be struggling with anxiety, fear, and guilt, symptoms that seemed consistent with the aftermath of a traumatic event. During one particular session, Erik, who was known to be more emotionally sensitive than his brother, broke down and confessed to the murders. Lyle, more controlled and assertive, confirmed the confession. They admitted to having killed their parents, describing their actions in chilling detail.

Dr. Oziel, caught between his professional obligations and the disturbing reality of the confession, faced a moral and legal dilemma. His sessions with the brothers were protected by doctor-patient confidentiality, but the severity of the crime weighed heavily on him. Unsure of how to proceed, Dr. Oziel took an unconventional and risky step: he recorded his sessions with the brothers, capturing their confessions and discussions about the murders on tape. These recordings would later become a key piece of evidence in the legal proceedings against Lyle and Erik.

Further complicating matters, Dr. Oziel shared his concerns with his mistress, Judalon Smyth. Fearful for his own safety after hearing the brothers' detailed confessions, Oziel confided in Smyth about what the Menendez brothers had told him. This disclosure set off a chain of events that would ultimately break the case wide open. Smyth, aware of the heinous nature of the crime, made the decision to contact the police and inform them of the confessions. Her tip gave investigators the leverage they needed to obtain the taped recordings of the brothers' therapy sessions.

With this information, the police now had concrete evidence linking Lyle and Erik directly to the murders. The confession provided the missing piece that the investigation had lacked up until that point. The once-insurmountable barriers of privilege, wealth, and status began to crumble, as the truth about the brothers' involvement in the crime came to light.

The Arrest – How the Brothers Were Finally Taken In

Armed with the information from Dr. Oziel's therapy sessions and the tapes, the police moved quickly to arrest Lyle and Erik Menendez. On March 8, 1990, nearly seven months after the murders, Lyle was apprehended at the family's Beverly Hills mansion. Erik, who had been away participating in a tennis tournament in Israel, received the news of his brother's arrest and decided to return to Los Angeles. Upon his arrival, he was met by law enforcement at the airport and taken into custody.

The arrests marked a dramatic shift in the investigation and public perception of the case. Up until this point, the brothers had maintained their public personas as grieving sons and beneficiaries of their parents' estate. Their abrupt apprehension cast them in a different light – not as victims, but as suspects in one of the most shocking crimes in Beverly Hills history.

Following their arrest, Lyle and Erik were held without bail, as the authorities feared they might attempt to flee the country, given their considerable financial resources. The brothers were charged with the murders of their parents, and the case against them was built on a combination of physical evidence, financial motives, and, most crucially, the taped confessions obtained from Dr. Oziel. The stage was now set for a legal battle that would captivate the nation.

As the news of their arrest spread, the media frenzy intensified. Reporters flocked to cover every detail of the case, broadcasting the brothers' privileged backgrounds and recounting the brutal nature of the murders. The Menendez brothers quickly became household names, and their faces were plastered across newspapers, television screens, and magazine covers. Public opinion remained divided: while some viewed them as cold-blooded killers motivated by greed, others saw them as products of a deeply troubled household, possibly driven to violence by years of alleged abuse.

The arrest of the brothers was a pivotal moment, transforming the case from a high-profile murder investigation into a legal spectacle. It was clear that the trial would not only examine the specifics of the crime but also delve into the complexities of family dynamics, wealth, and the psychology of privilege. Lyle and Erik Menendez, once anonymous heirs of a prominent family, were now at the center of a case that would challenge societal views on crime and justice.

Preparing for Trial – The High-Stakes Legal Strategies

The Menendez brothers' trial was set to be one of the most high-profile legal battles of the decade. From the outset, the defense and prosecution each crafted intricate strategies designed to sway the jury on what was shaping up to be a highly emotional and sensational case. For the prosecution, the goal was straightforward: to prove that Lyle and Erik Menendez had murdered their parents in cold blood, motivated by greed and the desire to inherit the family fortune. For the defense, however, the strategy required a more nuanced approach, one that delved into the brothers' upbringing and the alleged horrors they endured within the family home.

Lyle and Erik hired a legal team that included Leslie Abramson, a well-known defense attorney famed for her tenacity and skill in high-stakes cases. Abramson's strategy hinged on portraying the brothers as victims of severe psychological and sexual abuse at the hands of their father, José Menendez. The defense argued that this abuse had created a climate of fear and desperation, culminating in the brothers' decision to kill their parents. It was a risky move, hinging on the jury's willingness to empathize with the brothers despite the brutal nature of their crime.

To support this narrative, the defense planned to introduce extensive testimony about the alleged abuse, drawing on the brothers' own accounts as well as statements from family members and friends. This strategy was designed not only to explain the brothers' actions but also to evoke sympathy, suggesting that the murders were the result of years of accumulated trauma rather than cold, calculated greed. Leslie Abramson's approach was met with both skepticism and support, as it raised complex questions about the impact of familial abuse and the psychological pressures it could exert.

On the other hand, the prosecution, led by Deputy District Attorney Pamela Bozanich, sought to frame the murders as a premeditated act motivated by financial gain. They highlighted the brothers' lavish spending in the aftermath of the crime and presented the taped confession as a clear indication of their guilt. The prosecution argued that the brothers had carefully planned the murders, going so far as to purchase shotguns days in advance and concoct a false alibi. Their legal strategy was rooted in the assertion that Lyle and Erik were manipulative individuals who had killed their parents to secure their inheritance.

The trial preparations also involved a battle over what evidence would be admissible in court. The recordings made by Dr. Oziel were a contentious point, as the defense argued they were obtained in violation of doctor-patient confidentiality. The prosecution, however, maintained that the severity of the crime outweighed the confidentiality rules, especially given that the information had come to light through Smyth's tip to the police. The judge ultimately allowed the tapes to be used as evidence, providing the prosecution with a powerful tool to bolster their case.

As the trial date approached, public interest reached a fever pitch. The case, now deeply embedded in the national consciousness, was poised to explore not just the specifics of a heinous crime but also broader themes of wealth, family dynamics, and the justice system's treatment of privileged defendants. The stakes were high for both the defense and prosecution, as the outcome would hinge on convincing the jury of either the brothers' victimhood or their calculated malice. With both sides fully prepared for a grueling courtroom battle, the stage was set for a trial that would leave an indelible mark on legal history.

CHAPTER 5: THE FIRST TRIAL – JUSTICE OR MEDIA CIRCUS?

•

Trial Proceedings – Prosecution vs. Defense Arguments

The first trial of Lyle and Erik Menendez began in 1993, capturing the public's attention and sparking debates that extended beyond the courtroom. The proceedings were marked by a fierce clash between the prosecution and the defense, each presenting narratives that sought to sway the jury's perception of the brothers' motives. The trial soon became a battleground of arguments, evidence, and emotional testimonies, laying bare the complexities of the case.

From the outset, the prosecution maintained that this was a straightforward case of cold-blooded, premeditated murder. Deputy District Attorney Pamela Bozanich and her team argued that Lyle and Erik had meticulously planned the killings to inherit their parents' fortune. They highlighted the brothers' purchases of shotguns days before the murders and their staged alibi of going to the movies on the night of the crime. A key piece of evidence was the taped confession made during their sessions with Dr. Jerome Oziel, in which the brothers recounted the murder and their rationale behind it. The prosecution used these tapes to paint a picture of the brothers as calculating and manipulative, driven by greed rather than fear.

In contrast, the defense, led by attorney Leslie Abramson, presented a narrative steeped in trauma and emotional turmoil. They did not deny that Lyle and Erik had killed their parents; instead, they argued that the murders were the result of years of psychological, physical, and sexual abuse perpetrated by José Menendez. Abramson sought to frame the brothers as victims of an oppressive and terrifying household, claiming that the abuse had pushed them to a breaking point. According to this narrative, the brothers lived in constant fear for their lives, believing that their parents would eventually harm them if they did not act first.

To support their case, the defense called upon numerous witnesses, including family members, friends, and experts in abuse and trauma. Lyle and Erik themselves took the stand, delivering emotional testimonies about their father's alleged abuse and their mother's complicity. They described a household ruled by fear, detailing the relentless physical and sexual violence they endured from a young age. These harrowing accounts aimed to evoke empathy and to explain the brothers' actions as a desperate attempt to escape a life of torment.

The prosecution, however, sought to dismantle the abuse narrative. They argued that the brothers' testimonies were a fabrication designed to justify their actions and manipulate the jury. They pointed to inconsistencies in the brothers' accounts and emphasized their lavish spending spree following the murders as evidence of their true motive. The prosecution further contended that even if some abuse had occurred, it did not warrant the premeditated and brutal nature of the murders. The courtroom became a theater of emotional intensity, with both sides presenting arguments that challenged the jury to consider not just the facts of the crime but the psychological and moral dimensions involved.

Media Coverage – Turning a Trial into Entertainment

While the legal teams waged their battle inside the courtroom, an entirely different spectacle was unfolding outside. The Menendez trial quickly became a media sensation, with news outlets, talk shows, and tabloid magazines covering every detail of the case. The trial was one of the first to be broadcast live on Court TV, bringing the drama into millions of American homes and turning the proceedings into a form of entertainment.

The decision to televise the trial introduced a new dynamic to the case. Viewers were able to watch the courtroom unfold in real-time, witnessing the emotional testimonies of Lyle and Erik, the arguments from both legal teams, and the reactions of the jury and the judge. The presence of cameras transformed the trial into a national event, blurring the lines between legal proceedings and reality television. The public became engrossed in the brothers' story, dissecting every piece of testimony and forming opinions on their guilt or innocence based on what they saw on TV.

Media coverage often focused on the most sensational aspects of the trial: the dramatic revelations of abuse, the brothers' wealthy lifestyle, and the gruesome details of the crime scene. Headlines were crafted to provoke, painting the brothers alternately as tragic victims of a tyrannical father or as ruthless killers seeking wealth. Talk shows and news segments debated the case, with legal analysts and psychologists offering their interpretations of the brothers' motives and the strength of the prosecution's evidence. The trial was transformed into a cultural phenomenon, sparking discussions about wealth, privilege, and the complexities of family dynamics.

This intense media scrutiny had a significant impact on public perception. Many viewers were swayed by the emotional accounts of abuse, sympathizing with Lyle and Erik as victims of a traumatic upbringing. Others, however, saw the trial as an example of the justice system being manipulated by wealth and celebrity status. The televised nature of the trial also put pressure on all involved parties, including the jury, who now faced the added burden of knowing that their decisions were being watched and judged by the public at large.

The media's portrayal of the trial raised questions about the influence of public opinion on legal proceedings. Could a fair and impartial trial truly occur when the case had been so thoroughly dissected and sensationalized in the court of public opinion? These concerns became even more relevant as the trial progressed toward its dramatic conclusion.

The Hung Jury – Why the First Trial Ended in Mistrial

After months of testimonies, arguments, and public speculation, the first trial of Lyle and Erik Menendez concluded in January 1994. However, it did not end with the definitive verdict that many had expected. Instead, the trial concluded in a deadlock, resulting in a hung jury and a mistrial. The outcome stunned both the legal teams and the public, raising questions about the complexity of the case and the power of the brothers' defense strategy.

The deadlock was the result of two separate juries – one for Lyle and one for Erik – each unable to reach a unanimous decision on the charges of first-degree murder. In both cases, the jurors were divided, split between those who believed the brothers acted out of genuine fear for their lives and those who saw the murders as premeditated and financially motivated. The prosecution had pushed for a conviction on first-degree murder, emphasizing the evidence of premeditation and the brothers' calculated actions before and after the killings. The defense, on the other hand, had successfully introduced enough doubt into the minds of some jurors regarding the brothers' state of mind and the extent of their alleged abuse.

The jurors who leaned toward acquittal were swayed by the brothers' emotional testimonies and the accounts of abuse that painted a picture of a dysfunctional and terrifying household. They struggled with the question of whether the brothers' actions, though extreme, could be seen as a response to years of trauma and a genuine belief that their lives were in danger. Conversely, those who argued for conviction focused on the deliberate nature of the murders, the planning involved, and the brothers' subsequent behavior, which they interpreted as signs of guilt rather than relief.

The hung jury underscored the complexity of the case and the difficulty in separating the emotional elements from the legal standards required for a murder conviction. The mistrial highlighted how deeply the trial had polarized not just the jurors, but also the broader public. Some viewed the mistrial as a failure of the justice system to hold the brothers accountable, while others saw it as an acknowledgment of the complexities involved in cases of alleged familial abuse.

With the mistrial declared, the legal battle was far from over. The prosecution vowed to retry the case, determined to secure a conviction, while the defense prepared for another grueling fight. The stage was set for a retrial that promised to revisit the arguments, testimonies, and media spectacle that had already captivated the nation. However, the hung jury in the first trial had already set a precedent, illustrating just how challenging it would be to reach a consensus in a case so entangled with emotion, privilege, and the blurred lines between victimhood and culpability.

CHAPTER 6: THE RETRIAL – A DIFFERENT OUTCOME

Changes in the Retrial – What Was Different This Time?

The retrial of Lyle and Erik Menendez began in 1995, nearly two years after the conclusion of the first trial. The legal teams, the evidence, and the media circus returned to the courtroom, but with notable changes that would ultimately influence the outcome. This time, the proceedings unfolded with a stricter set of guidelines and a different approach by both the prosecution and the defense, setting the stage for a more decisive verdict.

One of the most significant changes in the retrial was the ruling that the trial would not be televised. Unlike the first trial, which had played out in the living rooms of millions of Americans, the retrial was kept behind closed doors, away from the public eye. This decision was made to reduce the potential for media influence on the jury and the trial's proceedings. It allowed the case to be presented in a more controlled environment, minimizing the spectacle and focusing attention on the legal aspects of the brothers' actions rather than on their personalities or public personas.

Another crucial change was the judge's decision to limit the defense's argument regarding the alleged abuse. In the first trial, the brothers had provided extensive testimony about the physical, emotional, and sexual abuse they claimed to have suffered at the hands of their father, José Menendez. This testimony had evoked strong emotional responses and had been a key factor in the jury's inability to reach a unanimous verdict. However, in the retrial, the judge ruled that the defense could not rely on the same extensive argument of "imperfect self-defense" as a justification for the murders. While evidence of abuse was still allowed, it was significantly constrained, with the focus shifting more toward the facts of the crime itself rather than the psychological state of the brothers.

The prosecution seized the opportunity presented by these changes. They streamlined their case, emphasizing the premeditation and brutality of the murders. They brought forward evidence of the brothers' actions in the days leading up to the crime, including the purchase of shotguns and the fabricated alibi, to demonstrate that the

killings were meticulously planned. The prosecution also stressed the brothers' extravagant
spending spree following their parents' deaths
as indicative of their true motive: greed and the
desire for financial freedom.

The defense, led again by Leslie Abramson,
faced an uphill battle in the retrial. With the
abuse narrative significantly limited, they had
to pivot their strategy, focusing on the brothers'
psychological state and the alleged fear they
lived in. However, without the extensive emotional testimonies that had previously swayed
some jurors, their case lost much of the impact
it had in the first trial. The retrial became less
about the emotional complexities of the Menendez family dynamics and more about the cold,
hard facts of the crime.

The Conviction – Life Without Parole

The retrial reached its conclusion in March 1996,
with both the prosecution and defense having
presented their final arguments. The jury, composed of individuals who had been screened
for impartiality and shielded from the intense
media coverage that had surrounded the first

trial, deliberated for several days. This time, they emerged with a unanimous decision that would change the course of the brothers' lives forever.

Lyle and Erik Menendez were found guilty of first-degree murder and conspiracy to commit murder. The verdict came as a decisive response to the central question of whether the brothers had acted out of fear or premeditation. The jury rejected the defense's portrayal of the murders as a response to years of abuse, instead accepting the prosecution's argument that the killings were a calculated act motivated by greed. The brothers' confessions, their detailed planning of the crime, and their behavior afterward solidified the jury's conviction that this was a case of cold-blooded murder.

The sentencing phase of the trial followed, with the jury deliberating whether the brothers should receive the death penalty. After much consideration, they opted for a sentence of life imprisonment without the possibility of parole. This decision reflected the gravity of the crime while also acknowledging the complexities presented during the trial. The verdict of life without parole ensured that Lyle and Erik would spend the rest of their lives in prison, bringing a sense of closure to a case that had captivated the nation.

For the Menendez brothers, the verdict marked the end of their lives as free men. They were transferred to separate prisons, a standard practice to prevent collusion between inmates convicted of the same crime. The once-privileged sons of a wealthy family were now inmates, facing the reality of life behind bars for the murders they had committed. The finality of the sentence underscored the consequences of their actions, cementing their place in American legal history.

Public and Legal Reactions to the Verdict

The verdict in the retrial elicited strong reactions from both the public and the legal community. Many viewed the outcome as long-overdue justice, a necessary response to a crime that had shocked the country with its brutality and its perpetrators' seeming lack of remorse. For those who had followed the case since the first trial, the conviction represented a sense of closure, an affirmation that the law had prevailed despite the complexities and emotional weight of the arguments presented.

The media, which had played a significant role in shaping the public narrative during the first trial, covered the retrial and its verdict with a more subdued tone. The decision not to televise the retrial meant that the proceedings did not generate the same level of public spectacle, allowing for a more sober reflection on the case's outcome. Some commentators lauded the retrial as a more impartial and fact-focused examination of the brothers' actions, noting that the limited focus on the abuse allegations had enabled the jury to concentrate on the premeditated nature of the murders.

However, not all reactions were supportive of the verdict. A segment of the public and some legal experts continued to express sympathy for the brothers, arguing that the years of alleged abuse and the psychological trauma they endured warranted a more lenient sentence. They questioned whether the legal system had adequately considered the impact of familial abuse on the brothers' mental state and whether life imprisonment was a just response to a situation that, in their view, had been shaped by extreme parental mistreatment.

The retrial and its outcome also sparked discussions about the legal treatment of abuse allegations in murder cases. It raised questions about how much weight such claims should carry when evaluating the motives and culpability of defendants. For some, the limited scope allowed for the abuse narrative in the retrial signaled a need for the justice system to more carefully balance the complexities of psychological trauma with the standards of criminal accountability.

In the end, the conviction of Lyle and Erik Menendez to life without parole became a defining moment in the case. It signaled a shift from the more sensationalist aspects of the trial to a legal resolution based on the evidence of premeditation and the brothers' motives. While public opinion remained divided, the legal system had rendered its judgment, closing the chapter on a crime that had forever altered the lives of the Menendez family and left an indelible mark on American culture.

CHAPTER 7: LIFE BEHIND BARS – THE MENENDEZ BROTHERS TODAY

Adjusting to Prison Life – From Wealth to Incarceration

For Lyle and Erik Menendez, the transition from a life of privilege and wealth to the harsh reality of prison was both abrupt and profound. The brothers, once accustomed to luxury and freedom, found themselves navigating the constraints and routines of the prison system. Following their sentencing, they were initially placed in different maximum-security prisons in California, a decision made to prevent any possible collusion between them.

Lyle was sent to Mule Creek State Prison, while Erik was incarcerated at the Richard J. Donovan Correctional Facility. Life in prison was a stark contrast to the opulence they had known. The Menendez brothers, now just two of thousands of inmates, had to adapt to an environment where their past wealth and status meant nothing. Their days became defined by the strict schedules and regulations of the prison system: early morning wake-ups, routine meals, and limited recreational time. The once-independent men now lived under constant surveillance, surrounded by the grim reality of incarceration.

Despite these conditions, both Lyle and Erik managed to adjust to prison life over time. They immersed themselves in various activities offered within the prison system. Lyle took on jobs and became involved in educational programs, earning a college degree during his incarceration. He found solace in helping fellow inmates, offering guidance and support, which gave him a sense of purpose. His engagement in these activities allowed him to find a semblance of normalcy and community within the prison walls.

Erik, similarly, sought to make the best of his situation. He involved himself in the prison's educational and self-help programs, focusing on mental health and personal growth. Erik found comfort in developing relationships with other inmates and participating in activities like gardening. For both brothers, the adjustment was not without challenges, but they managed to carve out roles for themselves within the prison environment, transforming their lives from the chaos and violence of their past into something more stable and structured.

After years of separation, a significant moment occurred in 2018 when Lyle and Erik were reunited at the Richard J. Donovan Correctional Facility. This reunion marked a turning point in their incarceration, allowing them to reconnect after decades apart. They now live in the same housing unit, providing each other with familial support in an otherwise isolating world. The bond they share has become a crucial aspect of their lives behind bars, offering them a source of strength as they continue to serve their sentences.

Marriages and Relationships Behind Bars

One of the more surprising aspects of the Menendez brothers' lives in prison has been their ability to form relationships, including romantic ones. Despite their life sentences without the possibility of parole, both Lyle and Erik have managed to find companionship, entering into marriages that have captured public interest and further complicated their narrative.

Lyle was the first to marry. In 1996, while serving his sentence at Mule Creek State Prison, he wed Anna Eriksson, a former model who had written to him after learning about his case. Their relationship developed through letters and visits, a form of connection that prison regulations allowed. However, their marriage did not last; Anna divorced Lyle in 2001, reportedly due to his continued focus on the legal battles and appeals.

Despite this setback, Lyle found love again. In 2003, he married Rebecca Sneed, a journalist who had initially corresponded with him regarding his case. This relationship, like his first marriage, developed through written communication and limited visits, adhering to the strict rules of the prison system. Lyle's marriage to Rebecca has endured, becoming a cornerstone of his life behind bars. Their relationship offers Lyle emotional support and a connection to the outside world, providing him with a sense of normalcy despite his circumstances.

Erik, too, found companionship while incarcerated. In 1999, he married Tammi Saccoman, a woman who had been following his case and had reached out to him. Their wedding ceremony was conducted in the prison, with strict regulations in place. Unlike Lyle, Erik has remained married to Tammi, and their relationship has been a source of stability for him. Tammi has been a vocal supporter of Erik, advocating for his case and maintaining a public presence to keep the brothers' story in the spotlight.

Both marriages have sparked fascination and controversy. Some view the relationships as a testament to the brothers' capacity for personal growth and the human need for connection, even in the most adverse conditions. Others, however, see them as an extension of the Menendez brothers' ability to attract attention and manipulate their narrative. Regardless of public opinion, these marriages have become integral to Lyle and Erik's lives in prison, providing them with emotional bonds that help them cope with the reality of their sentences.

Appeals and Ongoing Legal Efforts

Since their conviction, Lyle and Erik Menendez

have continued to pursue legal avenues to challenge their life sentences. Over the years, they
have filed multiple appeals, hoping to overturn
their convictions or, at the very least, secure
new trials. These efforts have involved both
the exploration of legal technicalities and the
revisiting of the central arguments related to
their alleged abuse.

One of the brothers' key legal strategies has
been to argue that their original trial was fun-
damentally flawed due to limitations on the
defense's ability to fully present the history of
abuse. Their legal team has contended that crucial evidence and testimony that could have
painted a clearer picture of their psychological
state and the context of their actions were either
dismissed or restricted during the retrial. They
argue that a new trial, with a more compre-
hensive consideration of the abuse allegations,
could lead to a different outcome.

Despite their persistent efforts, the courts have
been largely unresponsive to these appeals.
Both state and federal courts have upheld the
original conviction, ruling that the evidence
presented at the retrial was sufficient to support

the verdict of first-degree murder. The courts have maintained that the limitations placed on the defense's arguments during the retrial were appropriate, given the focus on the premeditated nature of the crime.

In recent years, however, the Menendez brothers have gained renewed public attention, partly due to documentaries, television series, and social media discussions that have revisited their case. This resurgence in interest has sparked debates about the justice system's handling of abuse allegations and the complexities of familial violence. Some advocates have called for a re-examination of the brothers' sentences, arguing that the nuances of their psychological state and the alleged abuse were not adequately addressed during the legal proceedings.

While the chances of a new trial or a change in their sentences remain slim, Lyle and Erik continue to explore every possible legal option. They have expressed hope that shifting public perceptions and evolving understandings of abuse might eventually influence the courts to reconsider their case. For now, they remain imprisoned, holding onto the possibility of a future where their story might take yet another unexpected turn.

CHAPTER 8: THE LEGACY OF THE MENENDEZ CASE

The Case's Impact on Discussions of Abuse and Justice

The Menendez case left an indelible mark on the public's perception of abuse, trauma, and justice within the family dynamic. At the heart of the brothers' defense was the claim that years of psychological, physical, and sexual abuse at the hands of their father, José Menendez, had driven them to a state of desperation and fear. This narrative introduced the broader public to the complexities of familial abuse, forcing society to confront the uncomfortable reality that violence and manipulation can exist behind even the most affluent and successful facades.

In the 1990s, discussions about domestic abuse, particularly within wealthy families, were not as openly addressed as they are today. The Menendez case brought these issues into the spotlight, highlighting how abuse could lead to tragic outcomes even in families that appeared to have everything. The brothers' testimonies during their trials, recounting the alleged horrors they faced, became a catalyst for conversations about how abuse can shape behavior and decision-making. Some viewed their actions as a grim result of their trauma, while others questioned the authenticity of their claims, suspecting a strategy to elicit sympathy and justify their crime.

The case also sparked debates about how the legal system handles abuse allegations, particularly when they intersect with violent crime. The limitations imposed on the defense's argument regarding abuse during the retrial raised questions about the extent to which such claims should be considered when evaluating criminal actions. Were Lyle and Erik victims acting out of fear, or were they murderers seeking to manipulate the system to evade accountability? This ambiguity continues to resonate in legal circles, where the balance between acknowledging past abuse and enforcing the law remains a topic of ongoing debate.

In more recent years, the Menendez case has been revisited in light of evolving attitudes toward mental health and trauma. Modern psychological research has shed light on the long-term effects of abuse, including how it can impact decision-making and self-perception. As society has grown more aware of these complexities, there has been a reevaluation of how cases like the Menendez murders should be understood. While the brothers' actions remain condemned, their story has contributed to a broader discourse on the psychological impact of familial abuse and the challenges in seeking justice in such contexts.

Media and Pop Culture – How the Case Continues to Fascinate

The Menendez brothers' story has endured not just in legal discussions, but also in media and pop culture. From the outset, the case captured public attention, thanks in large part to its dramatic elements: a wealthy family, brutal murders, allegations of abuse, and a pair of young, seemingly privileged defendants. This intrigue only deepened as the trials unfolded, providing a mix of courtroom drama, emotional testimonies, and sensational media coverage that riveted audiences.

Over the decades, the Menendez case has been revisited through documentaries, TV specials, true crime series, and even fictionalized adaptations. In 2017, the high-profile TV series "Law

& Order True Crime: The Menendez Murders" brought renewed focus to the case, exploring it from multiple perspectives and reigniting public interest in the brothers' story. Documentaries and true crime podcasts have continued to dissect the details, analyzing the evidence, legal strategies, and psychological aspects of the case. These media portrayals often reflect changing societal attitudes, offering nuanced takes on the brothers' motives and the implications of their actions.

Part of the case's enduring fascination stems from its dramatic elements, but it also taps into deeper questions about wealth, privilege, and the American justice system. The Menendez brothers were young, affluent, and seemingly destined for success. Their crime shattered the myth of the idyllic upper-class family, revealing a darker reality beneath the surface. This contrast between outward success and inner turmoil continues to captivate audiences, making the case a frequent subject of exploration in pop culture.

Moreover, the story's complexity has allowed for a range of interpretations. Some portrayals focus on the brutality and premeditation of the murders, casting the brothers as cold-blooded killers. Others emphasize the abuse narrative, inviting viewers to consider the psychological trauma that may have influenced their actions. This multiplicity of perspectives has kept the Menendez case relevant, ensuring that it remains a topic of discussion, analysis, and, at times, empathy.

Changing Perceptions – Modern Re-evaluation of the Brothers' Actions

As societal views on mental health, abuse, and the justice system have evolved, so too has the perception of Lyle and Erik Menendez. While they were initially viewed by many as ruthless killers motivated by greed, modern re-evaluations have prompted some to reconsider this simplistic characterization. Documentaries, interviews, and social media have contributed to a growing discourse that questions whether the brothers' actions can be fully understood without considering the psychological impact of their alleged abuse.

In recent years, a number of advocates and supporters have voiced their belief that the brothers deserve a second chance. This perspective stems from a broader understanding of trauma and its effects on human behavior. Those who support the Menendez brothers argue that the abuse they suffered, as described in their testimonies, created a psychological state in which they believed that violence was their only means of escape. For these advocates, the life sentences handed down to Lyle and Erik represent a failure to fully account for the complexities of their situation.

Social media has played a significant role in reshaping public opinion. Platforms like TikTok, Instagram, and Twitter have seen an uptick in discussions about the case, with some users expressing sympathy for the brothers and criticizing the justice system's handling of their trial. This online engagement has brought the Menendez case to a new generation, many of whom were not alive or were too young to remember the initial media frenzy of the 1990s. For these individuals, the story is viewed through the lens of contemporary understandings of abuse, mental health, and the nuances of criminal justice.

However, not all perceptions have changed. Many continue to view the brothers' actions as inexcusable, regardless of their upbringing or the abuse they claimed to have endured. They argue that the premeditation, brutality, and subsequent behavior of Lyle and Erik cannot be justified, and that their life sentences are a just consequence for their crime. This viewpoint underscores the ongoing tension in how society evaluates crimes involving family violence and mental health, highlighting the complexity of the Menendez case and its lasting impact on public discourse.

Today, Lyle and Erik Menendez remain in prison, their lives a stark contrast to the freedom and luxury they once knew. Yet, the legacy of their case continues to evolve. It serves as a touchstone in conversations about abuse, mental health, and the criminal justice system, reminding society that behind every sensational headline lies a deeper story of human experience, pain, and the quest for understanding. The Menendez brothers may forever be associated with their crime, but their story's influence ex-

tends beyond the confines of their cells, prompt-
ing ongoing reflection on the complexities of
family, trauma, and justice.

CONCLUSION

The Menendez brothers' story is one of tragedy, complexity, and lasting intrigue. From the brutal murders of their parents to the sensational trials and their subsequent lives in prison, Lyle and Erik Menendez have remained figures of public fascination for decades. The case has not only left a mark on the American justice system but has also sparked broader conversations about abuse, privilege, and the psychological impact of family dynamics.

In exploring their lives, actions, and the aftermath of the crime, it becomes clear that the Menendez case is far more than just a tale of murder. It is a story that forces society to grapple with difficult questions about the nature of justice, the influence of wealth and status, and the way trauma can shape a person's behavior. The brothers' actions were undeniably heinous, and the pain caused by their crime is immeasurable. Yet, their claims of abuse and the emotional complexities they presented during their trials have prompted ongoing debate about how such factors should be weighed in the pursuit of justice.

The case also highlighted the role of media in shaping public perception. The first televised trial captivated viewers, turning legal proceedings into a form of entertainment and influencing opinions on both sides of the case. This media spectacle blurred the line between justice and drama, leaving a legacy that continues to resonate in today's true crime culture.

Decades after the murders, Lyle and Erik remain behind bars, but the questions surrounding their case persist. Were they cold-blooded killers driven by greed, or were they victims of a toxic and abusive environment, pushed to the brink by years of trauma? Public perception has evolved, influenced by modern understandings of mental health and abuse. However, the case's complexities ensure that it defies simple categorization, leaving it open to interpretation and discussion.

Ultimately, the Menendez case serves as a reminder that behind every headline-grabbing crime lies a deeper narrative of human experience. It prompts reflection on the influence of family, the consequences of violence, and the challenges faced by the legal system in delivering justice. As the story of Lyle and Erik Menendez continues to be revisited and re-evaluated, it remains a powerful example of the enduring intersection between crime, psychology, and societal values.

WANT MORE IN A NUTSHELL?

Curious for more quick, engaging reads that make complex stories simple?

The *In a Nutshell* series offers concise, entertaining overviews of pop culture, history, and trending topics—perfect for readers who love to learn, laugh, and stay informed.

Explore the full *In a Nutshell* collection and discover other books and audiobooks by **Felix Grayson**, published by **MindSpark Publishing**.

Visit **FelixGrayson.com** to see what's new,

what's trending, and what's next.

FelixGrayson.com

Big ideas don't need big books.

Sometimes, the best stories fit perfectly—in a nutshell.

ACKNOWLEDGEMENT

I would like to express my gratitude to everyone who has contributed to the creation of this book. To those who have explored the complexities of the Menendez case over the years, your insights have been invaluable in piecing together this narrative. A special thanks to the researchers, legal experts, and journalists whose work has helped shed light on this multifaceted story. Finally, to the readers – your curiosity and willingness to delve into the complexities of this case drive the ongoing conversation about justice, family, and the human condition.

ABOUT THE AUTHOR

Felix Grayson has always been fascinated by the stories that shape our culture—from defining histor-ical events to the moments in pop culture that captivate millions. With a lifelong passion for storytelling and discovery, Felix brings clarity and insight to complex topics, making them accessible, engaging, and fun to explore.

As the creator of the *In a Nutshell* series, Felix combines thoughtful research with concise storytelling to deliver quick yet meaningful over-views of the people, events, and trends shaping our world. His mission is simple: to make learning enjoyable for everyone, no matter how busy life gets.

When he's not diving into the latest cultural phenomenon or uncovering forgotten chapters of history, Felix enjoys connecting with readers, sharing ideas, and exploring new stories—one nutshell at a time.

www.ingramcontent.com/pod-product-compliance
Lightning Source LLC
Chambersburg PA
CBHW020757130626
46554CB00006B/2238